Middle East Conflicts

Impact of Unstable Times

By

Dr. David K. Ewen

ISBN: 9798876061249
Imprint: Independently published by Enterprise College

Cover art by Emad El Byed via Unsplash

About the Book

This book delves into the contemporary conflicts that dominate today's Middle East headlines, offering readers a comprehensive understanding of their origins, current developments, and potential future trajectories. It serves as a guide to unravel the complexities of the region, providing insights into the historical context that set the stage for ongoing conflicts.

From the roots of these disputes to the present-day events shaping the Middle East, the book navigates through the intricacies of political, social, and cultural dynamics. By examining how these conflicts unfolded, readers gain a nuanced perspective on the factors contributing to the current state of affairs. The narrative not only explores the immediate causes but also delves into the historical underpinnings that have shaped the region's geopolitical landscape.

Furthermore, the book goes beyond mere analysis by offering a glimpse into potential future scenarios. By considering various factors and potential outcomes, it aims to equip readers with a forward-looking perspective on the Middle East. Whether it's the ongoing regional rivalries, internal strife, or international interventions, the book provides a comprehensive overview, fostering a deeper comprehension of the complexities at play.

About the Author

Dr. David K. Ewen is a distinguished professor of global communications studies, whose influence extends across continents, reaching students in Asia, the Middle East, Europe, Russia, and South America. With a rich academic background and a unique perspective on geopolitics, Dr. Ewen has become a significant figure in the field of global communication.

What sets Dr. Ewen apart is his distinctive perspective on geopolitics. He brings a nuanced understanding of the interconnectedness of global events and how communication plays a pivotal role in shaping the narratives surrounding them. His research often focuses on the intersection of media, politics, and culture, providing students with a comprehensive understanding of the complex dynamics that define our world.

In an era where the world is more interconnected than ever, educators like Dr. David K. Ewen play a crucial role in shaping the next generation of global citizens. Through his teachings and research, Dr. Ewen not only imparts knowledge but also fosters a deep appreciation for the complexities of global geopolitics and the vital role of effective communication in navigating this intricate landscape.

Table of Contents

Dr. David K. Ewen

Chapter 1: Escalating Tensions in the Middle East

The Middle East is currently grappling with heightened tensions that pose a serious threat of escalating into a wider and more devastating conflict. Recent military strikes conducted by the United States and the United Kingdom targeting Houthi rebels in Yemen have raised alarm bells about the potential for a larger war in the region. This comes amidst an already complex web of conflicts, including the crisis in Gaza and the multifaceted dynamics between various actors in the Middle East.

The escalating tensions are characterized by interconnected flashpoints, notably the conflict dynamics between Israel and Lebanon, the ongoing war in Gaza, and the activities of Iranian-backed militia groups. These developments have led to unprecedented levels of tension, sparking fears of a broader conflict that could have far-reaching consequences.

The potential for a wider conflict in the Middle East is not only a concern for the countries directly involved but also has significant implications for the global economy. The region's instability has already impacted global financial markets, with rising oil prices and increased geopolitical risks presenting substantial challenges to the world economy.

The crisis in Gaza further complicates the situation. The longstanding Israeli-Palestinian conflict has been a persistent source of tension, and recent escalations have strained relations even further. The Israeli government's response to rocket attacks from Gaza and subsequent military operations have resulted in civilian casualties, prompting international concerns about human rights violations. The situation in Gaza has the potential to not only fuel further unrest locally but also escalate tensions on a broader regional scale.

The involvement of Iranian-backed militia groups in conflicts across the Middle East adds another layer of complexity. Iran's support for proxy groups in countries like Iraq, Syria, and Lebanon has created a network of actors with diverse interests and alliances. The actions of these militias, coupled with their connections to Iran, have the potential to trigger wider conflicts and draw other regional and international powers into the fray.

Despite the alarming risk of a wider war in the Middle East, there are simultaneous and concerted efforts being made to prevent further escalation and avert a full-scale regional conflict. Several key players in the region recognize the profound implications such a conflict would have on economic, military, and political fronts. Consequently, there is a shared interest among these stakeholders to find diplomatic solutions and mitigate the potential fallout.

The realization of the economic, military, and political repercussions serves as a powerful motivator for regional actors to engage in efforts aimed at de-escalating tensions. A larger war could disrupt global oil markets, negatively impact trade routes, and exacerbate existing economic challenges. Moreover, the potential human cost and displacement resulting from a full-scale regional conflict are significant concerns that further incentivize diplomatic initiatives.

Diplomacy plays a pivotal role in these endeavors, with both regional and international actors actively working towards de-escalation and the pursuit of peaceful resolutions to the existing conflicts. Regional organizations, such as the Arab League, and international entities, including the United Nations, are involved in facilitating dialogues and negotiations. These diplomatic initiatives aim to address the root causes of the conflicts, promote understanding between conflicting parties, and formulate agreements that can lead to lasting stability.

In addition to diplomatic channels, there are likely backchannel communications and negotiations taking place to build trust and find common ground among conflicting parties. The complexity of the conflicts requires nuanced and multifaceted approaches that go beyond publicized diplomatic efforts.

The involvement of the international community in these diplomatic initiatives is crucial. Global powers, including the United States, the United Kingdom, Russia, and others, have a role to play in fostering dialogue and encouraging peaceful resolutions. The United Nations, with its mandate for international peace and security, can provide a platform for multilateral negotiations and contribute to conflict resolution efforts.

In the face of a precarious situation, the steadfast dedication to diplomatic solutions stands as a testament to the acknowledgment of the interconnected nature of global interests and a collective responsibility to avert a more extensive conflict. This commitment underscores the recognition that the repercussions of any escalation transcend regional boundaries, impacting the world at large.

The expressed hope is that ongoing diplomatic efforts go beyond merely addressing immediate conflicts; instead, they aspire to lay the groundwork for enduring peace and stability in the Middle East. This reflects an understanding that sustainable solutions require a comprehensive approach that considers long-term implications and addresses root causes, rather than focusing solely on immediate concerns.

Central to this approach is the emphasis on dialogue, negotiation, and collaboration. The passage highlights these elements as pivotal in navigating and resolving the intricate web of geopolitical challenges. By prioritizing open communication and cooperation, the intention is to create a framework that fosters understanding and consensus, ultimately paving the way for more effective conflict resolution.

The significance of these diplomatic efforts is further underscored by the recognition of the potentially devastating consequences of a full-scale regional conflict. Beyond the immediate human and material toll, such conflicts can have far-reaching impacts on the global stage, affecting economies, political stability, and international relations. Thus, the commitment to diplomatic solutions becomes a proactive measure to prevent the dire aftermath that could accompany a widespread escalation.

<ins>*Chapter 2: Israeli-Palestinian Conflict*</ins>

The Israeli-Palestinian conflict, particularly the ongoing battle in Gaza, continues to be a major source of regional instability. Each rocket fired and life lost adds to the already tense atmosphere in the area. The multinational involvement in the Yemen strikes further adds to the volatility. While these strikes were meant to curb Houthi attacks on shipping in the Red Sea, they have drawn condemnation and raised fears of further escalation. The intricate interplay of regional powers highlights the delicate nature of the situation, where a single misstep could have disastrous consequences.

The conflict has caused a humanitarian catastrophe and has the potential to lead to wider regional instability. The unfolding situation is having strong reverberations around the region, with concerns about potential violent disintegration and the impact on regional relations. A top United Nations official has warned that the risk of regional spillover of the Israeli-Palestinian conflict remains high, given the multitude of actors involved. It has become a truism that stability and security in the Middle East are inseparable from the resolution of the Israeli-Palestinian conflict.

The Israeli-Palestinian conflict has a long history of violence and political tension, with significant implications for regional stability. The conflict between Israel and Hamas, in particular, has led to devastating consequences and has the potential to draw in other regional actors, further exacerbating the situation.

The ongoing battle in Gaza is a distressing reminder of the persistent animosity between Israelis and Palestinians. The rockets fired by Hamas militants and the retaliatory airstrikes by the Israeli military have resulted in a tragic loss of life on both sides. The conflict not only affects the immediate area but also has far-reaching consequences for the entire region.

The involvement of multiple nations in the Yemen strikes adds another layer of complexity to an already volatile situation. While the intention behind these strikes was to protect shipping in the Red Sea from Houthi attacks, they have faced international condemnation and have raised concerns about the possibility of further escalation. The delicate balance of power in the region becomes evident as each action carries the potential for disastrous consequences.

The Israeli-Palestinian conflict has indeed led to a humanitarian catastrophe, resulting in significant implications for human suffering and regional stability. The ongoing violence has caused a staggering loss of life, with civilian casualties reaching unprecedented levels, and the destruction of civilian infrastructure, including hospitals and residential buildings. The conflict has taken a toll on the Palestinian people, with Gazan health officials reporting that the war has killed 10,000 Palestinians, including more than 4,000 children. The territory is also facing severe shortages of water, fuel, and supplies, as Israel has rejected humanitarian pauses and limited the amount of aid that can enter. This dire situation has created a desperate need for immediate action to address the humanitarian crisis.

Furthermore, the Israeli-Palestinian conflict has strained regional relations, with neighboring countries closely watching the conflict and expressing grave concerns about the potential impact on their own security. The conflict risks spreading beyond the borders of Israel and Palestine, as Israel exchanges missile fire with Hezbollah militants in Lebanon, strikes positions in Syria, and fends off occasional rocket fire from Yemen's Houthi rebels. The regional instability caused by the conflict has the potential to escalate further and create a wider crisis that could destabilize the entire Middle East.

To address the humanitarian crisis in the region, there is a need for an immediate ceasefire, unimpeded access for aid workers, and international humanitarian assistance. The international community has emphasized the importance of providing essential aid, water, food, and medicines to reach civilians who are suffering due to the conflict. The opening of crossings and guarantees of security for foreign nationals are also crucial steps in ensuring that humanitarian assistance reaches those in need. However, these efforts have been hindered by political complexities and the reluctance of involved parties to find common ground.

The resolution of the Israeli-Palestinian conflict and the achievement of stability in the Middle East require a new paradigm and a concerted effort from both regional and international actors to break the cycle of violence and ensure lasting peace. It is crucial to recognize that the Israeli-Palestinian conflict is not a simple issue with easy solutions. It is a complex and multifaceted problem with deep historical roots, political complexities, and religious disputes.

Understanding the complexities and nuances of the conflict is crucial in finding a sustainable solution that addresses the grievances and aspirations of both Israelis and Palestinians.

The Israeli-Palestinian conflict is indeed a matter of global concern, given its potential to cause wider regional instability. The delicate nature of the situation, coupled with the involvement of various actors, makes it imperative to find a peaceful and sustainable solution. This conflict, marked by a long history of violence and political tension, carries significant implications for regional stability. The risk of regional spillover remains high, and the involvement of multiple actors increases the potential for a full-blown conflict with devastating consequences.

It has become a widely acknowledged truth that stability and security in the Middle East are inseparable from the resolution of the Israeli-Palestinian conflict. The conflict's resolution demands a rights-based approach and a commitment to international law to ensure a just and lasting solution. According to the Carnegie Endowment for International Peace, a rights-based approach is crucial for conflict resolution in the Israeli-Palestinian context. This approach emphasizes the importance of human rights, equality, and justice for all parties involved. By centering rights and addressing the grievances of both Israelis and Palestinians, a sustainable solution can be found.

Similarly, the Lowy Institute highlights the Israeli-Palestinian conflict as the overriding issue in regional security. The unresolved conflict not only perpetuates violence and suffering but also hampers efforts to establish stability and cooperation in the broader Middle

East region. The conflict has far-reaching consequences beyond the borders of Israel and Palestine. The American University School of International Service points out that the conflict has implications for global security, with potential links to terrorism, radicalization, and the overall stability of the region.

The Council on Foreign Relations emphasizes the importance of U.S. policy in the Israeli-Palestinian conflict. As a major global power, the United States plays a significant role in facilitating negotiations and promoting a peaceful resolution. The conflict's complexity and sensitivity require a comprehensive and multilateral approach involving various international actors, as highlighted by the United Nations. The involvement of regional and global powers in supporting the peace process is crucial to ensuring its success and preventing further escalation.

Chapter 3: Middle East Power Dynamics

The recent events in the Middle East, particularly the conflict between Israel and Hamas, have highlighted the intricate challenges and risks that exist within the region's complex web of conflicts and power dynamics. This conflict has the potential to not only destabilize the Middle East but also the world at large. With various actors involved and the risk of drawing in neighboring countries such as Lebanon, the conflict forces international intervention and poses the risk of broader regional destabilization. Moreover, the conflict has had a profound impact on the geopolitical landscape, influencing regional stability and the foreign policies of various countries.

The Middle East has long been associated with high levels of armed conflict, but it is essential to recognize that the region's conflict dynamics are influenced by a multitude of intertwined issues. These include sectarian divides and competition over resources, which intensify one another and create a fertile ground for violence. At present, the Middle East is facing unprecedented levels of tension, with multiple flashpoints that could easily provoke a wider war. This precarious situation places the region on the verge of a potentially larger conflict.

The Israeli-Palestinian conflict is a deeply complex and longstanding issue that has far-reaching implications for regional stability and global security. At its core, this conflict is a result of a multitude of factors that have contributed to its escalation over the years. These factors encompass historical, political, and religious dimensions, making it a highly intricate and sensitive matter to navigate. The conflict centers around contentious issues such as the status of Jerusalem, Israeli settlements, borders, security, and water rights. Each of these elements carries immense weight and significance for both parties involved, further complicating the search for a viable solution.

Given the delicate nature of the Israeli-Palestinian conflict and the involvement of numerous actors, finding a peaceful and sustainable resolution is of utmost importance. It is imperative to address the grievances and aspirations of both Israelis and Palestinians in a just and fair manner. By doing so, a long-term peace agreement can be achieved, creating an environment of stability and prosperity not only for the Middle East but for the entire world.

One of the key reasons why resolving the Israeli-Palestinian conflict is crucial is to prevent further escalation and wider regional instability. The conflict has the potential to ignite deep-seated grievances and reanimate alliances across the region. This, in turn, could lead to an expansion of the conflict, causing a ripple effect with dangerous consequences. The stability and security of neighboring countries are intricately linked to the resolution of this conflict, highlighting the urgency of finding a sustainable solution.

The Israeli-Palestinian conflict has been a longstanding and complex issue that has attracted significant attention and efforts from the international community. Various parties, including Arab countries, the United States, and global organizations, have engaged in discussions and initiatives aimed at promoting peace between Israel and Palestine. Despite these efforts, the road to peace has been challenging and elusive.

Throughout the conflict, certain recurring themes have emerged as major obstacles to reaching a settlement. One such theme is the demand for a right of return by Palestinian refugees. This issue revolves around the desire of Palestinians who were displaced during the establishment of Israel to return to their ancestral lands. Finding a resolution that addresses the concerns of both Palestinians and Israelis on this matter has proven to be a significant challenge.

Another obstacle to peace has been Israeli settlement construction in the occupied territories. The expansion of Israeli settlements in the West Bank and East Jerusalem has been a contentious issue and a source of tension between the two sides.

The construction of these settlements, considered illegal by the international community, has complicated negotiations and created obstacles to the establishment of a viable Palestinian state.

Violence perpetrated by Palestinian militants has also been a major impediment to peace. Acts of terrorism and attacks targeting Israeli civilians have fueled mistrust and further strained the already fragile relationship between Israelis and Palestinians. These acts of violence have not only caused immense suffering but have also hindered efforts to build trust and find common ground for a peaceful resolution.

The failure to reach a settlement cannot be attributed solely to the actions of the parties involved. Broader political factors and failed negotiating paradigms have also played a significant role. The deeply entrenched positions and longstanding grievances on both sides have made it difficult to find common ground and reach a mutually acceptable solution. The international community's attempts to mediate and facilitate peace talks have often been met with limited success, as the underlying issues and complexities of the conflict prove challenging to overcome.

Israeli leaders have made repeated attempts to achieve peace, with the concept of a two-state solution serving as a central framework for negotiations. However, despite these efforts, the conflict persists, and the path to a lasting peace agreement remains uncertain. The Israeli-Palestinian conflict is deeply rooted in historical, religious, and territorial disputes, making it a complex issue that requires comprehensive and sustainable solutions.

In conclusion, the Israeli-Palestinian conflict is a deeply complex issue with significant implications for regional stability and global security. Finding a peaceful and sustainable solution is paramount to prevent further escalation and wider regional instability. Resolving the conflict in a just and fair manner can contribute to long-term peace, stability, and prosperity in the Middle East and beyond. It requires continued international efforts, empathy, and a commitment to understanding the historical, political, and religious dimensions that have fueled this conflict for decades. Only through a collective and genuine desire for peace can the Israeli-Palestinian conflict be resolved and a brighter future for all parties involved be achieved.

Chapter 4: Balancing International Relations

The international community often faces a delicate balancing act when dealing with conflicts and great power competition. This is evident in various global scenarios, such as the response to the US-China great power competition, Georgia's diplomatic balancing act between Russia and the West, Qatar's efforts to maintain a balancing act in its relations with Israel and Hamas, and the West's diplomatic balancing act in the Israel-Hamas war).

In the realm of international relations, maintaining a balance of power and preventing the ascent of a potential dominant force involve two primary strategies: balancing and buck passing. Balancing entails aligning one's power with that of another nation or group, achieved through bolstering one's own capabilities or enhancing the strength of allied nations. This strategy aims to counteract the power of potential aggressors, thereby ensuring stability in the international system. Balancing can be executed through internal or external means, such as strengthening a state's economic resources and military might.

On the flip side, buck passing refers to transferring the responsibility of handling a potential aggressor to another state. Instead of directly confronting a rising power, certain states opt to shift the burden of managing the threat to a different state. This approach involves fostering diplomatic ties with the aggressor, maintaining a reserved relationship with the "buck-catcher" state, increasing military strength to deter the aggressive state, and facilitating the growth of power in the intended buck-catcher. The balance of power theory posits a continual rebalancing of power among nation-states to prevent the emergence of an absolute power, known as a hegemon. This theory is observable in both historical and contemporary international relations, where nations strive to match and counterbalance each other's power to avert hegemony.

In the context of the Middle East, examples abound of states employing both balancing and buck-passing strategies to navigate regional power dynamics and thwart the rise of a hegemon. For instance, Turkey and Iran have been observed adopting these strategies in various regional contexts. Furthermore, the notion of passing the buck in the Middle East extends to external powers, such as China, playing a role in the region's power dynamics and security issues. These examples underscore the integral role of balancing and buck passing in the strategies employed by states to manage power relations and prevent the emergence of a dominant hegemon in the intricate geopolitical landscape of the Middle East.

States may choose to pass the buck in order to avoid direct confrontation or to divert the attention of the aggressor to another state. This can involve seeking good diplomatic relations with the aggressor, maintaining cool relations with the "buck-catcher" to avoid being dragged into a war, increasing military strength to deter the aggressive state, or facilitating the growth in power of the intended buck-catcher).

The complex and delicate nature of international relations requires careful navigation and strategic decision-making. Missteps in handling conflicts and great power competition can have significant consequences. Strategic decision-making involves anticipating and preventing violent conflict, as well as achieving locally-driven political solutions to stabilize regions. It also involves considering the interests and perspectives of various actors involved in the conflict and maintaining diplomatic relations to prevent further escalation.

Chapter 5: Journey Toward Global Stability

The U.S. Strategy to Prevent Conflict and Promote Stability is an important framework that outlines the goals and approach of the United States in fostering peace and stability globally. The strategy recognizes the need for a long-term, evidence-based, whole-of-government effort that integrates diplomacy, development, and security-sector engagement.

The goals of the U.S. Strategy to Prevent Conflict and Promote Stability are centered around prevention, diplomacy, development, and security-sector engagement. Prevention involves establishing and supporting capabilities to engage in peacebuilding and anticipating and preventing violent conflict before it erupts. Diplomatic engagement is crucial in fostering unity of purpose and collective action to broker and support political solutions. Development efforts are recognized as essential in addressing the root causes of conflicts and creating conditions for long-term peace and prosperity. Additionally, security-sector engagement is emphasized to promote stability and prevent conflicts by working with partner nations to strengthen their security sectors.

The strategy places great importance on peaceful resolutions and recognizes the devastating consequences of conflicts in terms of human lives lost and economic costs incurred. Diplomatic negotiations, mediation, and the pursuit of peaceful resolutions are seen as vital in addressing the root causes of conflicts and creating conditions for long-term peace and prosperity.

By actively engaging in efforts to prevent conflict and promote stability, the international community, including the United States, aims to break the costly cycle of fragility and promote peaceful, self-reliant nations that can become economic and security partners. The changing nature of conflict and violence, with conflicts becoming less deadly and often waged between domestic groups rather than states, highlights the increasing importance of efforts to achieve peace and stability in the international community.

One of the key aspects of this strategy is the emphasis on the role of diplomacy in preventing conflicts. Diplomatic negotiations are seen as crucial in resolving disputes and preventing them from escalating into full-blown conflicts. Mediation is also highlighted as an effective tool for resolving conflicts, with the United States actively engaging in mediating efforts around the world. By facilitating dialogue and bringing conflicting parties together, mediation can help find common ground and promote peaceful resolutions.

In addition to diplomatic efforts, the U.S. Strategy to Prevent Conflict and Promote Stability recognizes the importance of development in preventing conflicts. The United States Agency for International Development (USAID) plays a significant role in providing expertise and funding to improve development outcomes in areas affected by conflict and violence. By addressing the underlying socio-economic issues that often contribute to conflicts, such as poverty, inequality, and lack of access to basic services, development initiatives can help create more stable and resilient societies.

Furthermore, the strategy highlights the importance of security-sector engagement. By working with partner countries to strengthen their security apparatus and build their capacity to address security challenges, the international community can contribute to preventing conflicts and promoting stability. This involves training and equipping security forces, supporting good governance and the rule of law, and promoting respect for human rights.

Conflict prevention and stabilization efforts are crucial for maintaining peace, stability, and prosperity in the Middle East and other regions affected by conflicts. These efforts involve various strategies aimed at addressing the root causes of conflict, facilitating dialogue between conflicting parties, and increasing the inclusion of marginalized groups in peacebuilding. By actively engaging in conflict prevention and stabilization measures, the international community aims to contribute to long-term peace, stability, and prosperity not only in the Middle East but also globally. These efforts are particularly important in the Middle East, which has been experiencing a remarkable spate of diplomacy, de-escalation, and normalization, leading to positive developments for the region's long-term stability and prosperity.

In the context of international relations, balancing and buck passing are the main strategies employed to preserve the balance of power and prevent the rise of potential aggressors. Balancing refers to the act of states aligning themselves with other states or forming alliances to counterbalance the power of a potential aggressor. On the other hand, buck passing involves passing the responsibility of countering a potential aggressor to another state, rather than taking direct action.

According to John Mearsheimer, a prominent offensive realist, states can take several measures to facilitate buck passing. These measures include seeking good diplomatic relations with the aggressor, maintaining cool relations with the state that is expected to counterbalance the aggressor, increasing military strength to deter the aggressive state, and facilitating the growth in power of the intended buck-catcher. Both balancing and buck passing strategies play a vital role in managing great power competition and maintaining stability in the Middle East and beyond. These strategies are employed to prevent the dominance of any single power and to ensure a more stable and secure international system.

While the Middle East is experiencing positive developments in terms of diplomacy, de-escalation, and normalization, the region also faces economic challenges and risks due to conflicts. These challenges highlight the importance of international efforts to prevent further escalation and stabilize the situation. Addressing economic challenges in the Middle East requires a comprehensive approach that goes beyond conflict resolution. Efforts to promote economic stability and prosperity should be integrated with conflict prevention and stabilization measures. This includes supporting countries in building durable mechanisms to resolve conflicts, undertaking difficult reforms, enhancing social cohesion, and mobilizing domestic resources for lasting peace, stability, and prosperity.

In summary, the U.S. Strategy to Prevent Conflict and Promote Stability, along with the efforts of the international community, underscores the importance of conflict resolution in achieving long-term peace and prosperity. By employing a comprehensive and integrated approach, including diplomatic negotiations, mediation, and strategic decision-making, the goal is to prevent the escalation of conflicts and maintain global stability. The recognition of the interconnectedness between diplomacy, development, and security-sector engagement is crucial in addressing the root causes of conflicts and creating conditions for sustainable peace and prosperity.

Chapter 6: Dialogue and De-escalation

The humanitarian crises in Yemen and Gaza are indeed urgent and require immediate attention. Both regions are facing severe humanitarian crises, with millions of people in need of essential aid and assistance. The situation in Gaza has been described as a "catastrophe" with a "horrific" humanitarian crisis that is heading toward famine. The death toll in Gaza has exceeded triple the toll Yemen reached in three years, and the region is facing a risk of genocide. The ongoing conflicts and hostilities have led to intensified suffering and raised concerns about a widening regional war.

The humanitarian situation in Yemen is undeniably dire, with a staggering number of people in need of assistance and protection services. According to estimates, approximately 21.6 million Yemenis are in desperate need of humanitarian aid. The ongoing conflict in the country has resulted in widespread displacement, food insecurity, and a collapsing healthcare system. Shockingly, the World Food Programme (WFP) reports that a staggering 17 million Yemenis are food insecure, and 3.5 million pregnant and breastfeeding women as well as children under the age of five are suffering from acute malnutrition. This crisis has made Yemen one of the world's largest humanitarian crises, with the United Nations Children's Fund (UNICEF) reporting that 12 million children are in dire need of food, water, shelter, and medicine.

The situation in Yemen is a complex combination of factors, including the protracted conflict, economic collapse, natural disasters, and the impact of the COVID-19 pandemic. These factors have disproportionately affected women and girls, as the healthcare system has virtually collapsed, depriving them of essential sexual and reproductive health services. Consequently, there is a high risk of negative birth outcomes and malnourished infants, with over 1.5 million pregnant and breastfeeding women projected to suffer from acute malnutrition by 2023.

The conflict that has been ongoing in Yemen since 2015 has significantly exacerbated the humanitarian crisis in the country. This conflict has resulted in the death of thousands of civilians and the internal displacement of 4.5 million people. Additionally, the country's infrastructure, including vital overland routes and airports, has been severely damaged. As a result, Yemen's economy has shrunk by more than half since the conflict's onset, pushing the country to the brink of economic collapse.

Food insecurity is a major issue in Yemen, with 17 million Yemenis facing crisis levels of food insecurity. Both the World Food Programme (WFP) and the Food and Agriculture Organization of the UN (FAO) have identified Yemen as one of the acute food insecurity hotspots, where food insecurity is expected to remain at critical levels. The war has disrupted the supply chains for staple foods and basic goods, leading to skyrocketing prices for wheat and grain. Consequently, the hunger crisis in Yemen has worsened significantly.

Malnutrition rates among women and children in Yemen are among the highest in the world, with 1.3 million pregnant and breastfeeding women suffering from acute malnutrition. The situation continues to deteriorate, with nearly one-third of families having insufficient access to essential food items. The high rates of malnutrition pose significant risks to the health and well-being of women and children in Yemen.

The conflict and economic crisis in Yemen have severely impacted access to basic services such as safe water, sanitation, and healthcare. Millions of children lack access to safe water, sanitation, and hygiene services, resulting in regular outbreaks of communicable diseases like cholera, measles, and diphtheria. The collapsing healthcare system has further exacerbated the challenges faced by the population, particularly women and girls.

The international community has recognized the severity of the crisis in Yemen and has been providing humanitarian assistance to address the situation. The World Food Program (WFP) has launched its largest emergency response in Yemen, aiming to reach 15 million of the most vulnerable people with emergency food assistance in 2023. The United Nations Children's Fund (UNICEF) has also been working tirelessly to provide humanitarian assistance to the children in Yemen. Furthermore, the European Union (EU) has been supporting the United Nations Humanitarian Air Services (UNHAS) to ensure that aid workers can access the field and provide assistance to those in need in Yemen.

The conflict in Yemen, which has been ongoing for nine years, has pushed the country to the brink of economic collapse and has significantly impacted the well-being of its population. The war has led to the displacement of millions of people and has disrupted essential services, including healthcare and education. Natural disasters and climate-induced events, such as drought and flooding, have also contributed to displacement and heightened existing needs in Yemen.

The impact of the COVID-19 pandemic has further exacerbated Yemen's economic crisis and increased the risk of famine The pandemic has strained the country's healthcare system, making it even more challenging to provide essential services to the population. The economic downturn caused by the pandemic has also led to increased food insecurity and limited access to basic necessities.

Various organizations, including the World Food Program and UNICEF, are providing emergency food assistance, malnutrition screening, and other forms of support to the affected population in Yemen. The European Union has allocated significant humanitarian aid to assist those affected by the conflict in Yemen, focusing on the most vulnerable and disadvantaged. The coordinated response of the humanitarian community has prevented a catastrophe in Yemen, but the situation remains critical, and urgent action is needed to alleviate the suffering of the affected population and prevent a large-scale famine.

The United States has been urged to prioritize de-escalation in the region and to support efforts to address the humanitarian crises in Yemen and Gaza. Unimpeded access for aid workers and a cessation of hostilities are crucial to ensure the delivery of essential aid and assistance to those in need. It is important for all parties involved to prioritize dialogue and diplomatic channels to find lasting solutions to the underlying issues in the region.

The international community has a responsibility to respond to these urgent crises and provide the necessary support to the affected populations. Humanitarian organizations, such as the United Nations and non-governmental organizations, are working tirelessly to provide aid and assistance on the ground. However, their efforts are often hindered by the ongoing conflicts and limited resources.

In addition to immediate relief efforts, it is crucial to address the root causes of the humanitarian crises in Yemen and Gaza. This includes addressing the political, economic, and social factors that have contributed to the instability and suffering in these regions. It requires a comprehensive approach that focuses on peacebuilding, reconciliation, and sustainable development.

Furthermore, accountability for human rights abuses and violations of international humanitarian law must be prioritized. Perpetrators of violence and those responsible for obstructing humanitarian aid must be held accountable to ensure justice and prevent future atrocities.

The international community must come together to provide the necessary resources and support to address the urgent needs of the affected populations in Yemen and Gaza. This includes increasing funding for humanitarian aid, facilitating access for aid workers, and advocating for a peaceful resolution to the conflicts. Only through collective action and solidarity can we alleviate the suffering and ensure a better future for the people of Yemen and Gaza.

Chapter 7: Cooperation for Lasting Peace

Resolving the tensions in the Middle East is a complex task that demands the collective effort of both regional and international actors. The involvement of key players in diplomatic efforts and peace negotiations is crucial in finding a sustainable solution. The Arab League, consisting of countries like Qatar and Saudi Arabia, has actively engaged in mediating the Palestinian-Israeli conflict, striving to bring both parties to the negotiating table.

The United Nations (UN), the United States, and European countries, particularly the European Union (EU), have played significant roles in diplomatic initiatives and peace processes in the Middle East. These efforts are geared towards addressing the conflicts and promoting peace in the region.

The European Union maintains strong political and economic relations with partners in the Middle East, including Israel, the Palestinian Authority, Lebanon, Egypt, and Jordan. These relations are strengthened by Association Agreements and European Neighborhood Policy Action Plans. The EU's participation in the Middle East Quartet, alongside the United States, United Nations, and the Russian Federation, allows for collaborative efforts in addressing the conflicts. By working together, these entities can pool their resources and expertise to find peaceful solutions. The EU also engages in regular consultations with key countries such as Jordan, Egypt, Saudi Arabia, and the UAE, as well as the Arab League, to enhance the prospects for peace.

The United States has been actively involved in the Middle East peace process for many years. It has played a key role in brokering agreements and facilitating negotiations between Israel and its neighboring countries. For instance, the Camp David Accords in 1978 led to a peace treaty between Egypt and Israel, which was signed in 1979. In recent years, the United States has been involved in diplomatic initiatives such as the Abraham Accords in 2020, which led to the normalization of diplomatic ties between Israel and several Arab states. The United States' diplomatic efforts demonstrate its commitment to promoting peace and stability in the Middle East.

The United Nations has also been engaged in efforts to promote peace in the Middle East through various resolutions, peacekeeping missions, and diplomatic initiatives. The UN has played a crucial role in addressing the Israeli-Palestinian conflict and supporting the establishment of a two-state solution. It has facilitated negotiations and peace agreements between Israel and its neighboring countries. The UN's involvement provides a neutral platform for dialogue and helps bring conflicting parties together to find common ground.

The involvement of the United Nations, the United States, and European countries, particularly the European Union, has been instrumental in advancing the peace process in the Middle East. Their collective efforts, along with other key countries and organizations, enhance the prospects for peace in the region. By maintaining strong political and economic relations, participating in collaborative initiatives, and providing practical and financial support, these actors contribute to the ongoing efforts to address conflicts and promote lasting peace in the Middle East.

The involvement of these diverse actors is essential for building trust, fostering cooperation, and addressing the root causes of the conflicts. The conflicts in the Middle East are multifaceted, involving a complex interplay of local and international actors. Their engagement in conflict management practices may differ in form and structure, but a comprehensive approach encompassing a wide range of regional and international stakeholders is necessary to prevent further escalation and pave the way for a better future in the region.

The causes of conflicts in the Middle East are indeed complex and intertwined. They can be attributed to a combination of factors, including religious, ethnic, and cultural differences, competition for vital resources like water and oil, and the legacy of Western colonization.

The Middle East is a region with diverse religious, ethnic, and cultural groups. These differences have contributed to tensions and conflicts in the region. The presence of multiple religious beliefs, such as Islam, Christianity, and Judaism, has been a source of contention and conflict. The competing interests and ideologies of these different groups have often led to clashes and violence.

The Middle East is known for its significant oil reserves and its serious issues with water consumption. The competition for these vital resources, both locally and internationally, has been a major source of conflicts in the region.

Control over oil resources has often led to geopolitical rivalries and power struggles. Additionally, water scarcity and disputes over water rights have fueled tensions between countries in the region, such as the conflict between Israel and its neighbors over the Jordan River.

The legacy of Western colonization has had a lasting impact on the Middle East. The region's borders were drawn by Western powers following World War I, often disregarding the existing religious, ethnic, and cultural divisions. This has created tensions and conflicts among different groups within the region. The imposition of Western values, systems, and governance structures has also contributed to a sense of resentment and resistance among the local populations.

The Middle East has a turbulent history, with ongoing tensions and conflicts. International events such as the 9/11 attacks and the Iraq War have further exacerbated these tensions. The Israeli-Palestinian conflict, rooted in rival claims to the area between Jordan and the Mediterranean, is another significant source of conflict in the region. The unresolved nature of this conflict and the deep-seated grievances on both sides continue to fuel violence and instability.

It is important to note that the causes of conflicts in the Middle East are multifaceted and can vary depending on the specific context and region within the Middle East. The factors mentioned above provide a general understanding of the complex nature of these conflicts. However, it is crucial to acknowledge that each conflict has its unique dynamics and underlying factors that contribute to its escalation and perpetuation.

The conflicts in the Middle East have significant economic implications, affecting various sectors such as tourism, trade, investment, and overall economic stability. A large-scale conflict in the region would pose a major economic challenge, not only for the countries directly involved but also for neighboring countries and the broader Middle East and North Africa region.

The potential consequences of Middle East conflicts on neighboring countries like Egypt, Jordan, and Lebanon include disruptions in trade and investment flows, increased security risks, and the displacement of people seeking refuge from the conflict zones. These countries may also experience economic downturns due to reduced tourism and trade activities. The spillover effects of conflicts can be felt beyond the immediate conflict zones, affecting regional stability and global economic interconnectedness.

It is important to recognize that the economic implications of conflicts in the Middle East are significant and can have far-reaching effects beyond the immediate conflict zones. Efforts to resolve conflicts and promote peace in the region should take into account the economic dimensions and strive to create conditions for sustainable economic development.

Chapter 8: Economic Impact of Conflict

The economic impact of conflicts in the Middle East has been profound and far-reaching, affecting both the region and the global economy. The destruction of vital infrastructure, displacement of millions of people, disruption of trade routes, and damage to critical industries such as agriculture, oil production, and tourism have significantly hampered economic development and stability in the region.

One of the major consequences of Middle East conflicts is the rise in oil prices. These conflicts have led to increased geopolitical tensions and uncertainty, which in turn have affected oil production and supply. As a result, oil prices have climbed, adversely affecting economies worldwide. Higher oil prices can lead to higher inflation rates and increased production costs in various industries.

The conflicts in the Middle East have indeed had a significant impact on neighboring countries and international aid organizations due to the influx of refugees. The displacement of millions of people has put a strain on resources and redirected attention and resources away from other pressing global issues. The refugee crisis resulting from the conflicts in the Middle East have had transformative impacts on the politics, economies, societies, and states of the countries affected by forced population movements. The economic costs of intense conflicts and human displacement have been massive and persistent. Countries such as Iraq, Libya, Syria, and Yemen have experienced deep recessions, inflation, worsened fiscal and financial positions, and damaged institutions. These harmful effects have also spilled over into neighboring countries like Lebanon, Jordan, Tunisia, and Turkey, as well as other regions, notably Europe.

Neighboring countries have shouldered a significant burden in hosting large numbers of refugees. For example, by late 2022, over three-quarters of Syrian refugees resided in neighboring countries, including Turkey, Lebanon, and Jordan. The strain on resources and infrastructure in these countries has been substantial. Providing adequate shelter, healthcare, education, and other basic services for such a large population has proven to be a tremendous challenge. Moreover, the sudden influx of refugees has also strained the social fabric of these countries, leading to increased competition for jobs and resources, social tensions, and even conflicts.

The displacement of millions of people has also affected international aid organizations. These organizations have had to redirect their attention and resources to provide assistance and support to the affected populations. Humanitarian organizations have been working tirelessly to provide food, water, shelter, healthcare, and education to those in need. This redirection of resources has sometimes come at the expense of addressing other pressing global issues, diverting funds and manpower away from initiatives aimed at poverty alleviation, climate change mitigation, and other critical areas. As a result, the conflicts in the Middle East have had a ripple effect, impacting not only the immediate region but also the broader global community.

The challenges posed by the refugee crises require ongoing attention and support from the international community. It is essential for neighboring countries to receive assistance in dealing with the strain on their resources and infrastructure. International aid organizations need continued support to ensure they can effectively provide for the needs of the displaced populations. Additionally, there is a need for diplomatic efforts to resolve the underlying conflicts and create conditions for safe and voluntary return of refugees to their home countries. Only through collective efforts can we address the impacts of the conflicts in the Middle East and mitigate the strain on neighboring countries and international aid organizations.

Furthermore, the ongoing instability and insecurity in the region have discouraged foreign businesses from investing, leading to a stagnation of economic growth. The lack of investment hampers job creation and economic development, further exacerbating the economic challenges faced by the region.

Resolving these conflicts and investing in rebuilding efforts is crucial for promoting stability, fostering economic growth, and improving the lives of millions of people affected by these conflicts.

In conclusion, the economic impact of Middle East conflicts has been profound, with implications for both the region and the global economy. The destruction of infrastructure, displacement of people, disruption of trade routes, and damage to critical industries have significantly hampered economic development and stability. The rise in oil prices, influx of refugees, and lack of foreign investment have further compounded the economic challenges faced by the region. Resolving these conflicts and investing in rebuilding efforts is crucial for promoting stability and fostering economic growth.

Dr. David K. Ewen

Middle East Conflicts

Impact of Unstable Times

By

Dr. David K. Ewen

Middle East Conflicts

Impact of Unstable Times

By

Dr. David K. Ewen